.IEP and Section 504 Team Meetings – and the Law

Miriam Kurtzig Freedman, M.A., J.D.

www.SchoolLawPro.com
Boston, Massachusetts

*Together—moving from confusion to confidence
to the mission of educating ALL students!*

The information provided herein is intended to be used for general information only. It is not provided as legal or other professional advice or as a legal service. In the event that legal advice is required, services of an attorney should be sought.

Table of Contents

You're kidding! Another law book for educators and parents! We've had enough!

But wait! **IEP and Section 504 Team Meetings—and the Law** is different. It's quick. It's fun. It bridges the gap between educators (and parents) and lawyers. It answers the following important question:

What do educators and parents need to know and do to conduct meetings that are legal and efficient, build positive relationships, and get the job done?[1]

This *LITTLE LAW BOOK* is an antidote for the complexity surrounding these issues. We need to clarify requirements—so educators can get back to their classrooms, parents can get back to being parents, and, most important, students can get back to learning.

---

[1] These meetings have different names in different states. In this book, the term "Team meeting" is used for both IEP and Section 504 meetings. Check your state's practice!

Before we get to the law, let's ask these basic questions:

- Why have meetings?
- What purpose(s) do they serve? And not serve?

School personnel need to understand what Team meetings are, and what they are NOT—long before sending out meeting notices.

And, they need to understand how to steer these meetings aright when they go off course.

Ready? Almost!

One final thought before we start. Let's not get overwhelmed. Here, we deal with law only—not politics, education, or the latest trends. We learn what schools have to do—not whether the laws are good or the best way to teach. We leave those discussions for another day.

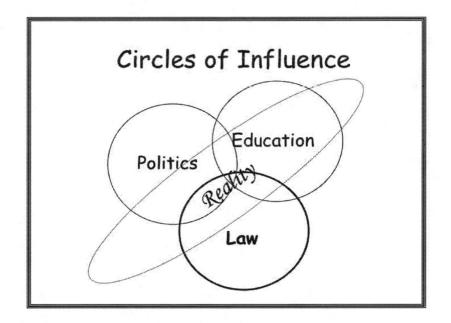

Circles of Influence

Politics

Education

Reality

Law

The special education law, the Individuals with Disabilities Education Improvement Act (IDEA), and the anti-discrimination law, Section 504 of the Rehabilitation Act of 1973 (Section 504 or simply, 504), each have different purposes.

The **IDEA** requires schools to develop Individualized Education Programs (IEPs) for eligible students[2] with disabilities (SWD).[3]

Section 504 requires schools to accommodate eligible SWD. Over the years, schools have come to develop written "504 plans" to document the services and accommodations they provide. Recall that while written "504 plans" are not legally mandated, they are often considered to be a "best practice." Thus, it's a good idea to have 504 plans in writing.

Remember the adage, *"If it's not in writing…. it didn't happen."*

---

[2] The words "child/children" and "student/students" are used interchangeably herein.
[3] See list of acronyms at the back of this *little book*.

First, what is the purpose of an IEP Team meeting?

An IEP Team's job is to, (a) develop an IEP that is "reasonably calculated to provide educational benefit" to the child and, (b) provide parents the opportunity to participate (more on this later). For the child, the Team's job is to write an IEP that provides a FAPE—a free appropriate public education.

Board of Education of the Hendrick Hudson Central School District v. Rowley, (1982).

But what is a FAPE?

Let's look at the letters—F. A. P. E. What does each stand for?

F—Free to the parents

A—Appropriate; providing an educational **benefit** for the child

P—Public; under public control, even if services are in a private setting

E—Education

More about the letters A and E!

A is for "appropriate."   But what is "appropriate?"

Again, check **_Rowley_**. The law provides a "basic floor of opportunity" for students with disabilities. The IEP needs to be "reasonably calculated to enable the child to receive educational **benefits**."   Schools are not required to "maximize the potential of each handicapped child."

Here, "benefit" is a noun—the IEP provides *a benefit*. The student will learn skills and knowledge and will progress. For most students today, the benefit is to learn academics in the general curriculum.

The next question is: how much benefit does the IEP need to provide?

Courts use different adjectives to answer this question, such as *meaningful, measurable,* or *some* benefit. All agree: the benefit needs to be more than trivial or *de minimis*. On the other hand, it does not need to be a maximum benefit; i.e., it does not need to be the best program for the child.

To demonstrate the benefit the child is to receive from the program, IEPs need to include measurable annual goals. They need to include the child's "present levels of academic achievement and functional performance" and appropriate "measurable" goals to demonstrate (show, prove) progress. Issues of what makes goals "measurable" go beyond this *little law book.*

For example, the 1st Circuit used the term "measurable benefit." **Roland M. v. Concord School Committee** (1st Cir. 1990).[4] The 6th Circuit famously used the car analogy. IEPs are to provide students with a serviceable Chevrolet, not a Cadillac. ***Doe v. Board of Education of the Tullahoma City Schools*** (6th Cir. 1993).

The Chevy must run well. It can't be a lemon. It need not be a Cadillac!

---

[4]   The United States is divided into 11 Circuit Courts of Appeals. These Courts hear appeals from lower courts, such as District Courts, and, from time to time, their decisions are appealed to the Supreme Court. See map of the Circuit Courts below.

E is for "education." But what is "education?"

The IDEA speaks about "academic achievement and functional performance" in many places; e.g., 20 U.S.C. Sec. 1414 (d)(1)(A).

Some states define education broadly—to include academic, emotional, social, behavioral, and physical needs. See, e.g., **_Mr. I. v. Maine School Administrative District No. 55_** (1st Cir. 2007). The Court found that "educational performance" is more than academics. The student with Asperger's Syndrome generally had strong grades, but had difficulty in "communication," an area of educational performance listed in Maine's law, making her eligible for special education services.

 Other courts focus on academics—the 3 R's, science, social studies, etc.

See, e.g., **_Hood v. Encinitas Union School District_** (9th Cir. 2007). Parents' reimbursement claim for private school placement is denied because student with SLD is not eligible for special education services. Prior to her removal from public school, the student consistently received average or above-average grades, even though she had an impairment. She did not need special education to learn in school.

OSEP has also chimed in. **_Letter to Clarke_** (OSEP 2007). OSEP writes, "[T]he Department's position that the term 'educational performance' as used in the IDEA and its implementing regulations is not limited to academic performance."

See discussion below for difference between an "impairment" and a "disability."

Check court decisions in your state and Circuit Court of Appeals,
as well as state laws and regulations.

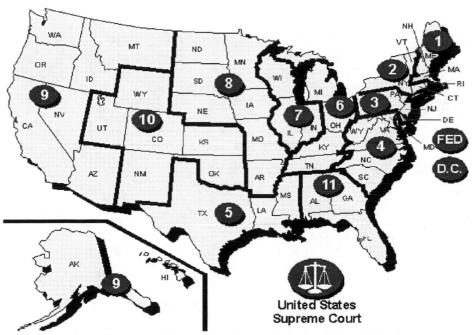

http://www.usdoj.gov/usao/eousa/kidspage/circuit.html

Let's discuss the "appropriate" standard a bit more.
Among issues that may arise at IEP meetings are the following:

1.   An argument may be made that the IEP is inappropriate because the gap between the student and her peers is widening (not closing). Courts have been unsympathetic to that argument, as the purpose of an IEP is to provide a meaningful benefit—not to pass state tests, close gaps, or meet NCLB standards. See *Derek B. v. Donegal School District* (E.D. PA 2007), *Leighty v. Laurel School District* (W. D. PA 2006), *Pierce v. Mason City School District* (S.D. OH 2007), *Houston Independent School District v. Bobby R.* (5th Cir. 2000).

2.   A Team member, such as a parent, advocate, or outside evaluator, may argue for a specific methodology, different from what the school proposes. However, it is long established that schools have authority to select the methodology, so long as it provides a FAPE. See *T. B. v. Warwick School Committee* (1st Cir. 2004), *Grim v. Rhinebeck Central School District* (2nd Cir. 2003), *G. D. v. Westmoreland School District* (1st Cir. 1991), *Lachman v. Illinois Board of Education* (7th Cir. 1988).

3.   A Team member may argue that because a student got an "F," he was denied a FAPE. The Team needs to consider why that happened. Was it lack of effort/failure to do work?   Was it the school's (LEA) failure to provide services? See, e.g., *Edinburg (TX) Consolidated Independent School District* (OCR 2007).

4.   And see discussion above about need for "measurable" goals.

PRACTICE HINT: Students with IEPs or 504 plans have the same opportunity to succeed or fail as other students.

IDEA eligibility determinations: Who needs an IEP?

Issues of eligibility and "child find" generally go beyond the scope of this *little book*. "Child find" is an affirmative duty that appears in the IDEA. 20 USC 1412 (a)(3).

It does not appear in the Section 504 law, but the OCR has incorporated into Section 504. "Child find" requires schools to identify, locate, and evaluate all children with disabilities in their jurisdictions. This affirmative duty is triggered if the district has reason to suspect a disability that causes the student to be unable to make effective progress in school (or, under Section 504, that "substantially limits" the student in a major life activity, such as learning).

Though these issues go beyond the scope of this *little book*, it may be helpful to cite some recent cases—when eligibility was not found, and when it was.

IEP NOT REQUIRED. _**Ashli and Gordon C. v. State of Hawaii**_ (D. HI. 2007). The Court upheld the LEA's decision that student with ADHD was not eligible for services. As part of regular education, teachers provided all students with differentiated instruction. The Court rejects parent's argument that the school should have considered the effects of ADHD on student's educational performance without considering the differentiated instruction in the class. If a student with an impairment can learn and perform in the regular classroom without specially designed instruction, the fact that his health impairment may have a (minimal) adverse effect does not render him eligible for special education services. See also _**Alvin Independent School District v. A.D.**_ (5th Cir. 2007), _**Hood v. Encinitas Union School District**_ (9th Cir. 2007), and _**Strock v. Independent School District No. 281**_ (D. MN 2008).

IEP REQUIRED. But see, _**Board of Education of Montgomery County v. S.G.**_ (4th Cir. 2007). Special education eligibility was found for a 15-year-old with schizophrenia because her emotional disturbance adversely impacted her educational performance. School was ordered to fund student's private therapeutic school. And see that First Circuit decision discussed above, _**Mr. I. v. Maine School Administrative District No. 55**_ (1st Cir. 2007).

PARENTS RIGHT. An IDEA FAPE also includes the parents' right to participate in the development of the IEP for their child.

Again, see the classic, **_Rowley_**: An IEP has to comply with "the procedures of the law," including providing parents with an opportunity to participate in the development of the IEP for their child.

It seems to us no exaggeration to say that Congress placed every bit as much emphasis upon compliance with procedures giving parents and guardians a large measure of participation at every stage of the administrative process...as it did upon the measurement of the resulting IEP against a substantive standard.

IEP Teams need to meet with parents and consider their views, requests, opinions, and information—and proceed in language parents can understand. Use plain language. Leave acronyms and jargon behind!

> PRACTICE HINT: If you do use acronyms, provide a list with definitions.

For IEPs, it's a good idea to remind Team members of the purpose of the IDEA:

...to ensure that all children with disabilities have available to them a free appropriate public education that emphasizes special education and related services designed to meet their unique needs and prepare them for further education, employment, and independent living.

20 USC 1400(d)(1)(A).

Second, what is the purpose of a 504 Team meeting?

As part of regular education, Section 504 plans are designed to provide eligible SWD the same opportunity to access, participate, and learn as their (average) non-disabled peers have. Such plans often include accommodations, services, therapies, and even, in rare cases, outside placements. They include whatever it takes to provide that opportunity.

Over the years, the OCR[5] has opined that Section 504 also provides a FAPE. Note, this requirement is not in the law—but is derived from years of practice in this field.

---

[5] Again, see list of acronyms in the Appendix.

A 504 FAPE differs from an IDEA FAPE!

Unlike the IDEA, Section 504 is an "opportunity" statute, not a "benefit" statute. See further discussion below.

> IEPs provide an educational benefit.
> 504 plans provide an equal opportunity.

504 Team members need to ask: how much opportunity is required? Answer: the same amount as **average** non-disabled peers need. Some people may argue for more and may wish to have a 504 plan to help a student meet her potential. However, Section 504 does NOT require that. Though not illegal, providing more than required "violates" the <u>Pyramid of Laws</u>, discussed below.

10 Similarities between IEP and 504 Team meetings

In preparing for any meeting, Team members need to understand what a FAPE is; what the job of the Team is—and isn't. And how Team meetings differ under these two laws. With that knowledge, the IEP and 504 Team will provide what is legally required—no more, and no less.

Team members need to know what the laws require, and what they do NOT require. See <u>Pyramid of Laws</u> below.

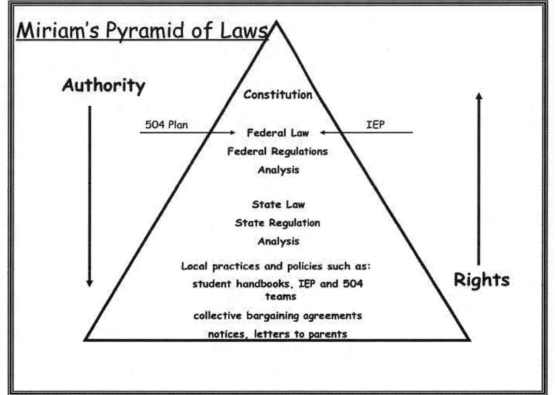

Miriam's Pyramid of Laws

Authority

Constitution

504 Plan → Federal Law ← IEP

Federal Regulations

Analysis

State Law

State Regulation

Analysis

Local practices and policies such as: student handbooks, IEP and 504 teams

collective bargaining agreements

notices, letters to parents

Rights

1. **Miriam's <u>Pyramid of Laws</u> helps Team members understand what the laws require and what goes beyond the requirements.**

Teams should provide what is necessary and required—not more or not less. They need to understand that if they do write too much into IEPs or 504 plans, those plans have to be implemented as written—even when they go beyond legal requirements, that is the legal *authority*. The <u>Pyramid</u> shows that *rights* go from bottom to top. Services that are included in IEPs or Section 504 plans, even if not legally mandated, rise to the level of federal law—like federal contracts.

Sometimes providing too much is not only unnecessary but has unintended side effects—"The Goldilocks Conundrum."™ These are discussed below.

2.   Both laws are based on "group think."

IEPs and 504 plans are based on Team decisions.[6] They are NOT developed by individuals—neither school personnel nor parents. Teams are groups of persons empowered to carry out two verbs:

First,	<u>CONSIDER</u> what the child needs.
Second,	<u>DECIDE</u> what the school will provide to meet those needs.

What does "consider" mean?

Consider means that the Team discusses, <u>reflects</u> upon, and <u>thinks</u> about, with a degree of care. It does NOT mean that the Team needs to adopt or follow what any Team member may request. Nor does it mean that every Team member must read every evaluation report or agree on all issues presented. A Team meeting is NOT a democracy, where everyone gets a vote and everyone's opinions count the same. Indeed, no vote should be taken! A Team meeting is the school's opportunity to offer services that will provide the child with a FAPE. No more. No less.

---

[6] With a new exception in the IDEA (2004), allowing schools and parents, by mutual consent, to make changes in an existing IEP without a meeting. 20 USC 1414 (d)(1)(D); 34 CFR 300.324 (a)(4)(i).

**G.D. v. Westmoreland School District** (1st Cir. 1991); _**T.S. v. Board of Education of the Town of Ridgefield**_ (2nd. Cir. 1993). Considering an independent educational evaluation (IEE) does not require a "substantive discussion." A Team member can summarize the IEE. The 8th Circuit determined that the requirement is met if the director of special education has read the IEE. _**Evans v. District No. 17**_ (8th Cir. 1988).

See also **L. M. v. Department of Education, State of Hawaii**, (D. HI 2006), where the District Court found that the school had considered (but not adopted) the parents' request. **A "veto" is not the same as failure to consider or to predetermine** a placement. _A great slogan!_

Unfortunately, many practitioners and parents are still confused about the meaning of this little word, "consider."

3. **Both IEP and 504 Teams can end ("have closure") without consensus; i.e., without having everyone in agreement.**

This is because an IEP and a 504 plan is the school's proposal—not a compromised document. In both types of meetings, it's a document designed to provide a FAPE—under the two standards of FAPE; i.e., the IDEA's and Section 504's.

See for example, **_Murray v. Montrose County School District_** (10th Cir. 1995), where the Circuit Court approved the IEP Team meeting's process.

Team members could not reach agreement. The school representative then made the placement decision at the meeting. The meeting ended. Was that OK to do? The Circuit Court said, YES.

Because the staffing team could not reach consensus on the appropriate placement for Tyler, the ultimate decision fell to Mr. Binder as the director of special education. (He was the representative of the public agency.)

4. IEP or 504 Team meetings are designed to provide what a student NEEDS, not what a parent WANTS.

IEP and 504 meetings are about what the student NEEDS, not what the student (or parents) may WANT. Remember the Rolling Stones' 1969 lyrics...

"You can't always get what you want....
And if you try sometime, you find you get what you need!"

Jefferson County School District R-1 (SEA CO 2003). Parent sought a laptop for the student with dysgraphia to take home after school. Hearing officer found it was a "want," but not a "need," and did not order it.

Park v. Anaheim Union High School District (9th Cir. 2006). Court found related services **"beneficial,"** but not **"necessary."** They were NOT ordered.

5. Both meetings lead to a FAPE that belongs to the child, not the parents.

Letter to McKethan (OCR 1996) involves a common situation: a child is found eligible for an IEP but the parent wants the services on a 504 plan instead. The OCR found that once a student is eligible for IDEA services and an IEP is developed for that student, the parent couldn't compel the district to provide those services on a 504 plan instead of an IEP. 34 CFR 104.33. A rejection of IEP services is also a rejection of 504 services, since one way for districts to comply with Section 504 is compliance with the IDEA.

In plain English—It's the Team's job to determine what the student needs, not what the parents want, when that differs from the Team's determination. The parents' recourse is to reject the IEP and proceed from there—not to compel the district to change its IEP.

29

6. At both types of meetings, educators are the experts when it comes to teaching and learning.

To treat them as experts, it's helpful to focus on the WHAT and the WHO. The WHAT is the general curriculum, the standards, the requirements—i.e., WHAT students are to learn. The WHO is the child and his/her needs.

The WHAT

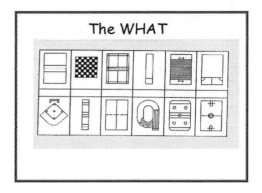

The WHO

| Each sport or game has its own rules, goals, etc. To play, you need to know them—the WHAT. | All children are unique. Each has his/her needs. The WHO is the child and his/her needs, etc. |

30

KEY: The 1997 IDEA reauthorization introduced (and the 2004 IDEA continued) the notion that most students with IEPs are to be included in the "general curriculum." Since then in IEPs, it's been first, the WHAT; then the WHO. Schools now need, first, to look at WHAT they teach in the general curriculum—then at how to include the student appropriately (the WHO). This has always been so under Section 504, which is a regular education service.

Remember: Educators are EXPERTS about the WHAT and the WHO. Parents and evaluators, about the WHO, but not the WHAT.

KEEP THE ROLES STRAIGHT!

31

Courts defer to educators who testify about their knowledge and experience with the student—as experts.

T.B. and E.B. v. Warwick School Committee, et al. (1st Cir. 2004). Parents lose a methodology challenge in a case about a seven-year-old child with autism. The court relied on the expertise of school personnel. It found that the district had *"well-trained teaching staff and a track record of success."*

PRACTICE HINT: DOCUMENT! DOCUMENT! DATA! DATA! DATA! How else did the Circuit Court know there was a record of success?

Watson v. Kingston City School District (2nd Cir. 2005). The Circuit Court upheld the district's IEP, which used a "comprehensive multi-sensory approach" for a student with a learning disability and rejected the parents' evaluators' recommendation for a private school, using Orton-Gillingham.

The mere fact that a separately hired expert has recommended different programming does nothing to change this, as deference is paid to the District, not a third party.

32

Heather S. v. Wisconsin (7th Cir. 1997).

*We note that the deference [cited in **Rowley**] is to trained educators, not necessarily psychologists. While the latter certainly have a role to play, and can contribute meaningful insight to the evaluation of a student, the school district is required to bring a variety of persons familiar with the child's needs to an IEP meeting, including, specifically, teachers.*

West Windsor-Plainsboro Regional School District Board of Education (D.C. N.J. 2005).

The Court critiqued the amount of deference given to the parents' outside "experts" by the administrative law judge. It found the parents' experts lacked credibility, especially as the chronology of the parents' prior decision to place their child privately affected the process. It reversed the hearing decision and found that the district had met its burden of providing a FAPE.

Alvin Independent School District v. A.D. (5th Cir. 2007). Interesting discussion of teachers' first hand knowledge of the child, in contrast to the physicians, who based their opinions on second-hand knowledge.

Leighty v. Laurel School District (D. W. PA 2006) and **_Jaffess v. Council Rock School District_** (D. E. PA 2006). These decisions provide excellent discussions of expertise in school personnel in describing the child's progress and benefit.

33

7. Inclusion—Team members need to know what it involves.

> <u>First</u>, they need to know the standards in the program—that is, the WHAT.
>
> <u>Second</u>, they need to know how to include this child appropriately. That is, how to educate the WHO.

More on the WHAT and the WHO

To do this, they need to know the difference between accommodations and modifications.

To get started, let's discuss what we will call the umbrella term that includes both accommodations and modifications—that is, "adaptations."

34

ADAPTATIONS

The **umbrella** term for **changes** in the IEP or Section 504 plan for a student with disability. These changes includes accommodations, appropriate accommodations, modifications, aids, benefits, and services. The term "adaptation" does not involve the concept of the effect of the changes on standards.

ACCOMMODATIONS/
APPROPRIATE ACCOMMODATIONS

Changes in course/test presentation, location, timing, student response, or other attribute which are **necessary** to provide **access** for a student with a disability to participate and demonstrate his "academic achievement and functional performance" and **do not fundamentally alter** or lower the standard or expectations.

MODIFICATIONS/
NON-STANDARD ACCOMMODATIONS

Changes in course/test presentation, location, timing, student response, or other attribute which are **necessary** to provide **access** for a student with a disability to participate and demonstrate ... (same as above....) but which **fundamentally alter** and/or lower the standard or expectations.

See _Grades, Report Cards, Etc...and the Law_ for a more detailed discussion of these important issues, including "The Goldilocks Conundrum,"™ discussed below. Please visit http://www.schoollawpro.com

36

A word about "252s." To determine eligibility OR services for an IEP or a 504 plan, Team members need to know what regular education already provides for all students, including SWD. Teams should not include 252's or "good teaching" services that are available for all students on IEPs or Section 504 plans.

Services in regular classrooms these days include **universal design** concepts, **scientifically-based instruction**, **response to intervention (RTI)** approaches, **differentiated instruction**, and other customized and individualized approaches for teaching all children. Dr. Perry Zirkel of Lehigh University dubbed some of these, "252's"—half of a 504! *A clever and helpful way to remember!*

252's do **not** belong on IEPs or 504 plans—as they are part of "good teaching."   They are neither "specialized instruction" nor adaptations, since they are available for ALL children.

Shelby County (TN) School District (OCR 2005). No need for an IEP or a Section 504 Plan, as the district provided classroom accommodations for all students. ***Community Independent School District*** (SEA TX 2004).   Regular education adaptations were appropriate. The student did not need special education or Section 504 protection.

The better regular education, the fewer IEPs and 504 plans are needed.

37

8. Some practices Teams need to avoid when providing a FAPE.

A. Beware of "The Goldilocks Conundrum."™ This is when Teams provide more than the child needs and ignore the side effects of doing so.

Usually, these extras are provided by people who mean well.

"Let's add this. It can't hurt."
Well, it can and often does.

Examples of The Goldilocks Conundrum™

- Providing too many adaptations and compensatory strategies—instead of teaching specific skills to the student.
- Overusing 1:1 aides. The student learns how to be helpless—called "learned helplessness."
- Providing inflated grades (perhaps based on effort, not achievement). These are a form of discrimination (as they are based on the child's disability—not class standards or expectations.)

39

For starters, see the following cases.

Fisher v. Board of Education of the Christina School District (DEL 2004) and **_Montgomery Township Board of Education_** (3rd Cir. 2005). Passing grades found to be based on overuse of accommodations and modifications, not the students' mastery of skills and knowledge.

Sherman and Nishanian v. Mamaroneck Union Free School District (2nd Cir. 2003). Court upheld school's refusal to provide a calculator that did all the functions being taught to the student. The school provided a less sophisticated model, so educators could determine what the student actually learned.

Axelrod v. Phillips Academy (D. MA 1999). The use of extended time was shown to be contra-indicated for the student. It did not help him organize his time. It was analogized to giving a later appointment to someone who is always late, when the student should be learning how to be on time!

J. L. v. Mercer Island School District (D. WA 2006). Too many accommodations masked the student's failure to learn basic skills. Two years in a private school ordered as compensation.

40

B.   Avoid "compromise" IEPs and 504 plans that try to make parents happy, BUT do not provide a FAPE to the student.

Goleta Union Elementary School District v. Ordway (D.C. CA 2002). The student services director changed the child's placement (at parent's request) without first assessing the placement. Later, the parent sued for Section 1983 money damages for violation of established law. The court allowed her to proceed.

Note: there is a split in the Circuit Courts of Appeals regarding the availability of money damage claims for IDEA violations.

Somoza v. New York City Department of Education (D. S. N.Y. 2007). The district provided a sham graduation and did other "good deeds" that lead to significant punishment of the district. Many cautionary tales here!

A 'good deed' may not be in the child's interest, as it may not provide a FAPE.

Sometimes, as the saying goes, _"No good deed goes unpunished."_

41

9. Team members need to know whose meeting it is!

Question: Is it the student's? the parents'? the district's?

ANSWER: It's the district's meeting, as the district is responsible for providing an IEP or a 504 plan. The meeting is the way it gets that job done.

Who runs the meeting? The district.

Who sets the agenda?   The district.

Who schedules it? The district.

Of course, the meeting proceeds at all stages (including scheduling) with input from parents, with due consideration of their requests and information.   That's why it's called a TEAM meeting!

42

Some specifics.

A.   Can parents request a meeting?   YES, of course.

B.   Can parents demand a meeting?

NOT under the IDEA or Section 504, though perhaps under state law. Under federal law, if the school does not believe a meeting is necessary, it does not need to schedule one.

- Under the IDEA, it needs to inform parents through <u>prior written notice</u> why no meeting will be held. The parents can dispute that decision, as they can any decision made by the district.

- Under Section 504, it needs to meet if the school has reason to believe the child may be eligible for 504 protection.

C.   Can parents demand that a meeting be scheduled at a specific time?

NO. Under the IDEA, the meeting needs to be jointly scheduled. Section 504 is silent on how to schedule meetings. Districts should develop and follow local policies and practices.

See below for discussion of the IDEA's Prior Written Notice.

43

10. Both types of meetings call for the use of plain language.

Team must assure that parents understand the Team process, the student's current academic achievement and functional performance, the services that are proposed, their options, etc. For evaluations under both laws and for IEPs, educators need to know the four attributes of parental consent or waivers for any process, evaluations, services, or placement, in which districts request parental approval. (Note that parental consent is NOT required in order to implement a 504 plan.) The consent or waiver must be:

1.	Voluntary
2.	Informed
3.	Written
4.	Revocable

See IDEA regulation, 34 CFR 300.9, and discussion of "consent" below.

Teams should:

- "Park" acronyms outside the meeting.
- Speak clearly and simply.
- Provide glossary for new terms; describe them explicitly.
- Offer to reconvene, if appropriate.
- Follow-up with the parents, as appropriate.

Examples of plain language:

Too complex—Don't use!   **Just right—Use!**

Too complex—Don't use!	Just right—Use!
Billy will participate in assessments.	Billy will take tests.
Billy has learned word attack skills.	Billy has learned to reads words.
The school affords Billy the opportunity to...	The school allows Billy... (Or, provides Billy...)
Billy will acquire knowledge.	Billy will learn.
I would appreciate if you would...	Please!

You get the idea! Keep it clear and simple!

46

Differences between IEP and 504 meetings

IDEA—a very prescriptive law. The law mandates who has to attend, when the Team needs to meet, how it should proceed, etc.

504—A much looser law. Every school district develops its own policies and practices.

First, let's discuss IEP meetings; then, 504 meetings.

IEP Team meeting: who, when, where, why, how

Who should attend?

Team Meeting Composition

- Parents of the Child
- Not less than 1 regular education teacher
- Not less than 1 SPED teacher
- LEA representative who is (1) qualified to provide/supervise provision of SPED and (2) knowledgeable about general curriculum and LEA resources
- Individual who can interpret instructional implications of evaluation results
- Others with knowledge or special expertise
- Whenever appropriate, the child

48

Some additional requirements. The IDEA also adds specific persons for meetings dealing with transitioning children from early childhood programs and for high school students transitioning to the next stage of their lives. 34 CFR 300.321 ((b)(1) and (f).

Finally, be sure that Team members understand the role of the LEA representative (who may or may not be the IEP Team chairperson).

The IDEA Regulations, at 34 CFR 300.321, define the role as:

> (4) A representative of the public agency who--
>   (i)   Is qualified to provide, or supervise the provision of,
>   specially designed instruction to meet the unique needs of
>   children with disabilities;
>   (ii) Is knowledgeable about the general education curriculum; and
>   (iii) Is knowledgeable about the availability of resources of the
>   public agency.
>
> (Authority: 20 U.S.C. 1414(d)(1)(B)-(d)(1)(D))

In sum, the LEA representative can provide or supervise special education, knows the general curriculum, and is authorized to create the plan and allocate resources.

49

Parental attendance—What the LEA needs to do to.

Districts are to "take steps to assure that one or both parents of a child with a disability are present at each IEP Team meeting or are afforded the opportunity to participate." Districts need to take specific steps and efforts to convince the parents to attend, and document their efforts. 34 CFR 300.322.

See, **_Mr. and Mrs. M v. Ridgefield Board of Education_** (D. CT 2007), where the district did not make necessary efforts to get the parents to attend. As a result, the District Court found a denial of a FAPE.

On the other hand, if a district takes steps to assure parental participation and parents still don't attend, the district can proceed without them to develop the IEP. This is long-established practice, consistent with the fact that it is the district's responsibility to provide a FAPE and the student's right to have the meeting and to receive services for a FAPE. See some recent decisions: **_E.M. v. Pajaro Valley Unified School District_** (N. D. CA 2007), **_E. P. v. San Ramon Valley Unified School District_** (N. D. CA 2007), **_Mr. G. v. Timberlane Regional School District_**, (D. N.H. 2007).

50

What if some school folks people don't attend?

That could be a significant issue. Courts seem to have focused attention on the requirement that the **regular education teacher** attend. Many courts find that if the teacher is not present for the discussion of the program, the parents were denied the opportunity to participate in the development of the IEP. Such may violate a free appropriate public education (FAPE). This focus by courts reflects the fact that providing parents with an opportunity to fully participate in the development of the IEP is the SECOND PRONG OF THE FAPE REQUIREMENT. Very important!

51

IEP Team members need to understand the role of the regular educator(s) at the IEP Team meeting.

34 CFR 300.320(a)(4).

To the extent appropriate:

- Participate in the development of the IEP for the child, including determining:

  o Appropriate positive behavioral interventions and supports
  o Other strategies for the child
  o Supplementary aids and services
  o Program modifications
  o Support for school personnel

Specific exceptions—excusals and waivers

The IDEA now allows Teams to get their work done in some situations when some members do not attend. Be cautious, however, in using these provisions.   34 CFR 300.321.

Excusing Attendance at Team Meeting

1. <u>Attendance Not Necessary</u>
2. <u>Attendance Necessary but Excused</u>

Both require written agreement with parent.

For necessary (but excused), excused Team member must submit written input to parent and other Team members <u>before meeting</u>.

53

To summarize,

For 1 above (attendance not necessary), the parents and school must **agree** that the person is not necessary.

For 2 above (necessary but excused), the parents must **consent**—a higher threshold.

Both the **agreement** in # 1 and the **consent** in # 2 need to be in writing. Remember the adage:

"If it's not in writing, it didn't happen."

Amending IEP Without Team Meeting

If:

- Parent and LEA agree not convene
- Team has already held annual meeting

Then:

May amend IEP with IEP amendment but must incorporate into IEP at parent request

20 USC 1414 (d)(1)(D); 34 CFR 300.324 (a)(4)(i).

The IEP Team needs to understand what parental consent is and why it matters.

This is an important issue under the IDEA (but not 504, unless required by state or local law or policy). Thus, unless local or state law requires it, schools do not need parental consent before implementing 504 plans. For IEPs, they do!   Educators need to bear in mind the IDEA definition of "consent." 34 CFR 300.9.

Consent means that--
    (a) The parent has been **fully informed of all information relevant**
        to the activity for which consent is sought, in his or her native
        language, or other mode of communication;
    (b) The parent **understands** and **agrees in writing** to the carrying
        out of the activity for which his or her consent is sought, and the
        consent describes that activity and lists the records (if any) that
        will be released and to whom; and
    (c)(1) The parent understands that the granting of consent is
        voluntary on the part of the parent and **may be revoked** at anytime.
    (2) If a parent revokes consent, that **revocation is not retroactive**
        (i.e., it does not negate an action that has occurred after the consent was given
          and before the consent was revoked). [emphasis added]

See above for the four attributes of parental consent and waivers.

56

Here is an example of a case where consent issues were violated.

**Somoza v. New York City Department of Education** (D. S. NY 2007). The parent, who was not represented by an attorney signed a waiver of rights as part of a settlement agreement. The District Court found that she did it not knowingly and not voluntarily. Thus, the waiver was ineffective! The Court also faulted the district for using a document that it had prepared unilaterally and whose language "was anything but 'clear and specific.'"

Consent and waiver issues—use care!

57

The IDEA's "prior written notice" requirement. Parents are entitled to know what the LEA is doing, not doing, and why.

The LEA needs to provide the parents with notice whenever it proposes to initiate a change or refuses to make a change about the identification, evaluation, educational placement, or FAPE for the child, that includes:

- A description of the action proposed or refused.
- An explanation of why the school is doing what it is doing.
- A description of other options considered and reasons they were rejected.
- A description of each evaluation procedure, test, record, or report the district used for its decision; other factors relevant to the district's decision.
- A statement of the parents' protection under the procedural safeguards of the law.
- If not an initial evaluation or referral, the way parents can obtain the procedural safeguards.
- Sources where parents can get help in understanding the law and their rights.

58

PRACTICE HINT! Wrightslaw, a parent advocacy/information website has the following anagram about smart IEPs—useful for parents and schools.

Goals on IEP need to be SMART: S— Specific
                                   M- Measurable
                                   A- Use Action words
                                   R- Realistic
                                   T- Time specific.

Source: SMART IEPs, From Emotion to Advocacy, 2nd Edition. www.wrightslaw.com.

Another smart reality is that school personnel should not stray beyond their area of expertise. This applies to descriptions of the child, current performance levels, recommendations, concerns, and so forth. For example, a speech and language specialist who attempts to "diagnose" depression or recommend psychotherapy—diminishes his credibility. Avoid that! Don't do it!

59

Since 2004, the IEP Team needs to consider the essential components of reading instruction that Congress added to foster explicit and systematic instruction. They are:

(A) phonemic awareness;
(B) phonics;
(C) vocabulary development;
(D) reading fluency, including oral reading skills; and
(E) reading comprehension strategies.

The IEP Team needs to consider "research-based instruction"

While IDEA 2004 does not define this term, the NCLB does—and the IDEA incorporates that definition.

"(A) research that involves the application of rigorous, systematic, and objective procedures to obtain reliable and valid knowledge relevant to education activities and programs; and

(B) includes research that-
(i) employs systematic, empirical methods that draw on observation or experiment;
(ii) involves rigorous data analyses that are adequate to test the stated hypotheses and justify the general conclusions drawn;
(iii) relies on measurements or observational methods that provide reliable and valid data across evaluators and observers, across multiple measurements and observations, and across studies by the same or different investigators;
(iv) is evaluated using experimental or quasi-experimental designs in which individuals, entities, programs, or activities are assigned to different conditions and with appropriate controls to evaluate the effects of the condition of interest, with a preference for random assignment experiments, or other designs to the extent that those designs contain within-condition or across-condition controls;
(v) ensures that experimental studies are presented in sufficient detail and clarity to allow for replication or, at a minimum, offer the opportunity to build systematically on their findings; and
(vi) has been accepted by a **peer-reviewed journal or approved by a panel of Independent experts** through a comparably rigorous, objective, and scientific review."
20 USC 7707(b) (37).

61

How do we do this at Team meetings?

Basically: Team members need to be able to answer these questions (essentially the same question):

"Why are you teaching my child in this way?"[7]

"Why are you using this method, approach, product, system, or…."

"How will your method help my child benefit? Tell me in plain language!"

In short, the IEP Team needs evidence that the program works and is based on "peer reviewed research to the extent practicable." This is especially so in proposing programs for teaching reading—as much research exists about that skill area.

And once in the IEP, be sure that the program is implemented with fidelity – that is, according to the specifications of that program.

---

[7] Thanks to Art Cernosia, Esq. for formulating this key question.

"With fidelity"

- Every day
- All the time
- Consistently
- Systematically
- Every day
- All the time
- You get the idea!

Some day-to-day practicalities at IEP Team meetings.

**A. The key requirement is to provide parents the opportunity
to participate meaningfully in the development of the IEP.**

It means that parents have the opportunity to share their views, information, and requests. It means that the Team considers these. The bottom line is that the parents had an opportunity to participate in the development of the IEP.

LEA's need to do what it takes to assure the above—including speaking in plain language, hiring a translator, hiring a "mentor" perhaps, etc.

On the other hand, it does not mean that the Team needs to take a vote or adopt the parents' opinion or preference.

64

And, it's a two-way street. **Parents need to be open about what they want and need to participate in the development of the IEP.**

Ellenberg v. New Mexico Military Institute (10th Cir. 2007). The parents never asked the Team for an IEP or requested that an earlier IEP be revised. Instead, they placed their child in a private school and sought reimbursement.   The Court dismissed their IDEA claim, as they had NOT exhausted the IEP Team process.

Similar result in ***C.G. and B.S. v. Five Town Community School District*** (1st Cir. 2008). The IEP was still being developed when the parents filed their due process complaint seeking payment for their unilateral placement.   The Court denied their reimbursement claim, as they had not cooperated with the Team process.

65

E.P. v. San Ramon Valley Unified School District, 48 IDELR 66, (N.D. CA 2007). Parents and their attorney made it clear that they would not agree to a Team meeting time or cooperate with the process. District went ahead and had the Team meeting in order to finalize the IEP for t he first day of school, even without the parents present. District did not violate the IDEA by proceeding with the meeting.

M.S. v. Mullica Township Board of Education (3rd Cir. 2008). The parent's refusal to cooperate with the Team process barred her reimbursement claim.

66

B. Be sure to provide the prior written notice.

See discussion above.   34 CFR 300.503(a)(1)(i).

See ***Independent School District No. 281 v. Minnesota Department of Education*** (MN App. Ct. 2007) (an unpublished decision), finding the LEA had violated the need for a prior written notice.   The Appeals Court rejected the district's argument that such notice was a mere technicality and ordered compensatory services.

67

C. School personnel can meet before the Team meeting.

In fact, a pre-Team "huddle" is often a good idea, so long as no decisions are made! After all, it is the Team meetings' job to **decide.** Pre-Team meetings can review data, progress reports, evaluations, options, opinions, etc.

**T. W. v. Unified School District # 259**, (10th Cir. 2005).

The Circuit Court found that school officials should come to the table with an **open mind,** but this does not mean they should come with an **"empty" mind.**

Another great slogan!

68

D. The district may come to meeting with a "draft" IEP.

So long as that "draft" is truly a "draft," is discussed and amended, as needed, at the Team meeting, and the parents' input is considered, etc.

See, ***Fuhrmann v. East Hanover Board of Education*** (3rd. Cir. 1993). In short—so long as it's truly a "draft."

In sum, consider a pre-IEP Team meeting if you need to:

- Clarify issues for the Team meeting
- Identify concerns that are known, both of of school personnel and of the parents
- Develop a "draft" IEP
- Be sure school personnel know what a FAPE is and what the Team process will be
- Be sure all members know that "consider" and "decide" are the operative words

70

E. **Team members may NOT make <u>decisions</u> before the Team meeting about what the school will offer.**

A resounding NO! Having Team members come to the meeting with a decision already made is an adamant "NO NO". It's called "predetermination" and violates the purpose and spirit of these meetings. Courts guard the Team process and often find "predetermination" to be a denial of a FAPE. Why so? Because the Team did not CONSIDER and DECIDE. Train staff on this!

<u>Deal v. Hamilton County Board of Education</u>, (6th Cir. 2004). Case about program predetermination for a student with autism. The parents sought ABA; the district had an eclectic program and the court determined that the district, having predetermined the placement, did not consider the parents' request. The decision dealt with procedural issues and was remanded to determine the substantive placement. See *<u>Deal v. Hamilton County Board of Education</u>* (6th Cir. 2008).

71

See also ***Winston-Salem/Forsyth County Board of Education*** (SEA NC 2005). And see ***Elmhurst School District 205*** (SEA IL 2006), where an Illinois hearing officer found the same, based on lack of discussion about placement options at the Team meeting, the Team's unwillingness to consider the home-based ABA program, and a computer generated IEP with another child's name in several places!

But see ***Hjortness v. Neenah Joint School District*** (7th Cir. 2007), where the Circuit Court rejected the parents' argument that the district predetermined the child's placement by not considering the private placement after the Team found the less restrictive public school placement appropriate. The Court found that the parents' rights to participate in the development of the IEP were not infringed in any meaningful way.

72

F. The least restrictive environment (LRE)—what do courts say?

The IEP needs to be in the LRE, so children with disabilities are educated with children who are not disabled, to the maximum extent **appropriate**. 20 USC 1412 (a) (5); 34 CFR 300.114.

LRE is a subject unto itself as standards continually shift. **Keep up with decisions in your state and Circuit!** In general, courts may weigh the benefits of inclusion in the general curriculum, the learning/progress that the child is reasonably expected to make, and the level of disruption the child may create in that classroom. Schools need to make efforts to include students in the school they would have attended if not for the IEP, collect data about that effort, make reasonable accommodations and modifications, and follow the mantra of providing a program where the child can receive a benefit. Some courts reason that schools do not need to set up parallel programs in regular classrooms that may be, as one court termed it, "beyond recognition." As a general rule, focus on the FAPE benefit test!

**Brillon v. Klein Independent School District** (5th Cir. 2004). The curriculum in regular education for the student was adapted "beyond recognition" ..."unduly burdensome," and not providing the student with educational benefit.

73

Pachl v. Seagren (8th Cir. 2006). The district's proposed program was upheld--a blend of separate programming and mainstream programming.

Clovis (CA) Unified School District (SEA CA 2006). 15-year-old student with mild to moderate mental retardation was properly placed in more restrictive special day class, not the parents' preferred vocational skills program at her local high school.

Board of Education of Township High School District No. 211 v. Ross (7th Cir. 2007). Student with Rett Syndrome did not receive meaningful educational benefit in the mainstream program. The LEA's proposed change of placement to a special education setting upheld. It is not enough to show that a student is obtaining some benefit, no matter how minimal, in the mainstream to prove that the LEA's removal of the student violated LRE.

Course level. Place students in appropriate academic levels. ***Middlesex Borough Board of Education*** (SEA NJ 2003). Moving a student to a lower level because she did not have "the math background" was not discriminatory when the student was unable to manage the work even with adaptations.

Timberlane Regional School District (SEA NH 2006). Hearing officer upheld district's proposed residential placement for a child with Type I diabetes, non-verbal learning disability, and a possible emotional disability.

74

And now we turn to the Section 504 Team meeting

The meeting is made up of a group of persons knowledgeable about three factors: the student, evaluation data, and the available resources.

Notice that federal law does not specifically mention the parents as 504 Team members. Check with your state law—in some they are. As **Miriam's Pyramid of Laws** above shows, states can provide more than the federal law, not less. Of course, it is generally good practice to include parents!

504 plans are designed to provide equal access for "otherwise qualified" individuals with a disability.

75

> ### Section 504 of the Rehabilitation Act of 1973 29 U.S.C. § 794 (A)
>
> - "No otherwise qualified individual with a disability...shall solely by reason of her or his disability, be excluded from the participation in, be denied the benefits of, or be subjected to discrimination under any program or activity receiving federal financial assistance."

An otherwise qualified individual is able to meet the **essential** requirements of the course, school—whatever. The law provides equal access, not advantage.

Cordiero v. Driscoll (D. MA 2007). A vocational high school did not discriminate against a student with Asperger's Syndrome when it did not admit him. Its admission policy was facially neutral and evaluated students on six criteria that this student did not meet.

Again, the WHAT ruled. It's all about the WHAT first. Then the WHO.

76

> **Section 504**
> **A "disabled person"**
>
> ...has a physical or mental **impairment** which **substantially** limits one or more **major** life activities, had a record of such impairment, or is regarded as having such and impairment, 29 U.S.C. § 706 (8)(B)

Section 504 plans are developed for students who have an impairment that substantially limits one or more major life activities. Note that they are not developed for students who are regarded as having an impairment or have a record of such an impairment. ***OCR Senior Staff Memorandum*** (OCR 1992).

When making Section 504 eligibility determinations, try using the baseball analogy, "running the bases." To be eligible for a 504 plan, a student needs to run the bases and get "home."

The analogy works because just about everyone knows the difference between getting to first, second, or third base—and getting home.

77

So, how does it work?

To get to first base—need an impairment.
To get to second base—need a major life activity (such as learning, breathing, walking, talking, seeing, working with one's hands, hearing, etc.). The life activities are global—not spelling or math or low self esteem.
To get to third base—need a limitation.
To get "home"—need the limitation to be substantial.

Only a student who "gets home" is eligible for a 504 plan.

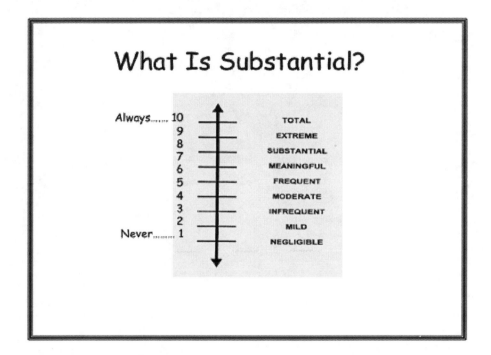

Thanks to Dr. Perry Zirkel for creating the model from which this has been adapted.

PRACTICE HINT: To make 504 eligibility determinations, separate the word "impairment" from "disability."

An **impairment** is a medical or psychological/ psychiatric/ educational diagnosis.

A disability is a legal conclusion made by the school-based 504 team. It's a judgment call, based on information about how the child is currently functioning.

An evaluator can provide expertise about the impairment. Parents can provide expertise about the child. Educators can provide expertise about the child and what the school is teaching. Only the Team can determine whether the child needs a 504 plan.

80

Bear in mind some attributes of Section 504 plans.

A. They are not supposed to provide an unfair advantage.

PGA Tour Inc. v. Casey Martin (2001). The Supreme Court allowed Casey Martin, the golfer, to use the golf cart as an accommodation. The Court reasoned, among other factors, that it did not give him an unfair advantage. If the cart had done so, the Court would not have allowed it.

B.   They include necessary services and adaptations that are not already provided by schools for all students.

See above discussion about "252s."

C. They do not provide "stay-put" rights.

There is no stay-put right under Section 504. This is an important difference from IEPs. As is the following.

81

D. 504 plans do not need to be accepted by parents.

504 plans provide services, such as accommodations, so the district does not discriminate unlawfully against an eligible student. The district does not need parental consent to do that under federal law. Check your state's laws and practices—as they may include such a requirement.

E. Parents have the right to dispute the district's action.

Parents have due process rights to dispute 504 plans through procedures set up by the LEA, the state, and/or the OCR. The LEA needs to inform them how to do this.

82

In summary, here are some NO's under Section 504

No's Under 504

- Impairment = Disability
- Boilerplate accommodations
- Too many accommodations
- Thinking there is "stay put"
- Including good teaching practices "252's"—thanks to Dr. Perry Zirkel--on 504 plans.
- Writing a 504 plan as a consolation prize

A Model 504 Accommodation Plan

Determining eligibility

1. Name of student; birth date; other identifying information

   _____

   _____

2. Members of the 504 team. And why each is there. What does each have knowledge about? (The child? Evaluation data? Placement options?) Be sure that each of these three types of knowledge is represented at the team.

   Name   Knowledgeable about

   _____

   _____

   _____

   _____

3. Sources of evaluation information. List each source. The plan does not require that each be summarized—just listed. In most cases, there should be more than one source; hopefully, some generated by school personnel who know the child.

   _____

   _____

4. List the physical or mental impairment by name. Again, no summary or description is required.

   _____

   _____

5. List the major life activity (ies) affected. Focus on the activity as a whole: i.e., learning—not math or writing; emotional impairment—not self-esteem

   _____

   _____

84

6. Quantify the degree of impact. On a scale of 1 to 10, is it about an 8? Use descriptors as mild, moderate, sometimes, and often—to find no eligibility; use descriptors as serious, substantial, almost always, etc.—to find eligibility. Compare the student to the average non-disabled student in the region (not, e.g. the average at a high achievement school.)

_____
_____
_____

Providing necessary accommodations

7. ACCOMMODATIONS: If eligibility is determined, decide what accommodations the student needs in order to have the same opportunity at school as his/her average nondisabled peers.

_____
_____
_____

8. SIGNATURES? NOT required. Often, it is good practice to have the parents sign to confirm that they received NOTICE of the 504 plan and their procedural rights under Section 504. Such rights give parents an opportunity to dispute the findings of the 504 team. Section 504 includes NO requirement that the parents consent to the plan. Thus, it is not advised to seek consent.

_____

CAVEAT: Parent signature(s) indicates that parents received NOTICE of the 504 plan developed for the child, and of their rights. Signature does NOT indicate parental consent or rejection, as Section 504 does NOT require parental consent in order to implement a 504 plan.

85

Good practices for both types of meetings

A. **Prepare for meetings.** *Preparation, preparation!*

- Invite the necessary participants.
- Prepare an agenda.
- Locate a comfortable room that is large enough for all. Is the table welcoming (like some water or a flower) or is it a mess (crumpled up papers, stacks of papers, etc.)? Make it attractive and welcoming. How about having some water available for all?
- Seat participants appropriately and, when needed, strategically. (Do we really need to sit in tiny chairs?)
- Prepare Team members before the meeting to understand the process, what FAPE is (and isn't), and their roles.

86

B. **Know the "cringe words." Don't use them at Team meetings.**

OOPS! I wish I hadn't said that!

- "We don't have that type of therapy here."
- "I don't know if we can do that. I'll check and get back to you."
- "I don't have time in my schedule to provide that service."
- "I'm not a psychologist, but I think Tom is depressed."
- "He needs 3 hours of therapy; but we can't fit it into our schedule."
- "I don't discriminate. I treat everyone exactly the same in my classes."

Keep the focus on the I in Individualized;
Never say Never!   Instead, say, "We'll consider it!"

87

C. Develop and follow an agenda and ground rules.

- If possible, get Team members' agreement with ground rules before meeting starts.
- Start and end on time!
- Do not allow interruptions or side conversations.
- Respect others; maintain confidentiality.
- Turn cell phones, pagers off. If expecting urgent call—inform Team members BEFORE the phone rings!
- Keep track of issues agreed upon—perhaps use flip chart or computer program.
- Announce when meeting is soon to end to allow members to wind down and discuss "next steps."

88

D.   Chair the meeting appropriately.

The Team leader or chairperson—

- represents the district, understands the process, and manages the personalities involved—keeping them focused on developing the plan
- sets out the purpose of the meeting, the "big picture"
- assists school personnel to be professional and cordial
- controls the meeting, takes caucuses or orderly breaks if appropriate
- paces the meeting and ends it on time. If need be, reschedules to complete the work

89

In short, the Team chairperson's job is to focus everyone's attention on the future—the plan that is being developed, not the past. Think of Wayne Gretsky, the great hockey player. When asked why he was so successful, he is said to have answered, "I skate to where the puck is going to be, not where it's been."

SO TOO HERE—FOCUS ON WHERE THE TEAM IS GOING AND WHAT THE STUDENT NEEDS—GOING FORWARD.

90

E. MOTHER WAS RIGHT! TEAM MEMBERS SHOULD FOLLOW HER SAGE ADVICE!

- Be on time! Don't keep parents and colleagues waiting.
- Start with friendliness. A smile always helps!
- Watch body language, especially rolling eyes, frowns, sighs, facial expressions, gum chewing, rudeness. Don't slouch! Make no promises you cannot keep.
- Follow up! Inform parents of their due process rights. Call or offer to meet with them to clarify confusion or concerns and to explain the process for mediation, due process hearing, etc. Return phone calls!

Work to build and maintain trust with families. Build positive relationships. After all, this is a relationship business!

91

F. What does a good meeting look like?

Agenda is followed.	Schedule is maintained. Meeting ends on time.
Chairperson exerts leadership.	Members are encouraged to be succinct, defuse challenging situations, and focus on the plan.
Members practice "active listening"—even when they dispute opinion of other(s).	Paraphrase, clarify, "I hear you saying that…"
Members acknowledge differences of opinion and the emotional nature of issues.	Use the "parking lot." Leave that issue for another time. Move on.
Members understand the basics, such as what a FAPE is—and isn't.	
Members learn how to deliver bad news—about grades, behavior, etc.	

92

G. What can go wrong at meetings   *WHAT IF ... WHAT TO DO*

Parents show up with an attorney—without having given prior notice to the school.	Give them the option of proceeding without the attorney or rescheduling meeting so both the parents' and school's attorneys can attend.
Parents bring a tape recorder without prior notice.	It depends on your state law and possibly local policies and procedures.
Tempers flare.	Take a short break. Set behavior expectations BEFORE the meeting. Do NOT tolerate intimidation or aggressive behavior! You may need to reschedule if Team members cannot act respectfully.
A Team member tries to take over.	Refer everyone to the written procedures. If member does not follow them, interrupt and rephrase what speaker is saying.
Team leader expects disruption.	Discuss contingencies in advance with administrators or security personnel.
Educator speaks outside area of expertise	Don't!
Participant cries, becomes emotional.	Acknowledge emotion. Take a break. If appropriate, end meeting and reconvene later.

93

And more things that can go wrong….

When conflict emerges—	Deal! That's the nature of the business. Don't ignore.
When parents and school disagree—	School representative decides. Remember, the meeting can close without consensus.
When the parents don't like each other and/or disagree with each other—	Stay neutral; don't take sides. Take a break if needed.
When conflicts emerge that are unresolved—	Say something like, "We need to move on. We need to agree to disagree."
When parents dispute Team decision—	Inform them of their due process rights, including mediation, resolution meeting, and hearing. Offer to meet them after meeting.
When agenda is not completed by the time the meeting is to end—	Reconvene; or, when appropriate, offer to meet with parents informally.

**Thank you to Nancy Kolb, Things that "Go Bump" in the Meeting.
Professional Development, CASE/EDCO/LABBB, Waltham MA.**

H. If you are really concerned about how the Team meeting will go—

Serve food! Make it welcoming and friendly. There's nothing like a nice glass of cold water or cup of hot coffee to ease tensions and create a more productive atmosphere.

I. After the meeting—

- Follow up. Contact parents to see if they have concerns or questions.
- Reconvene if circumstances change; e.g., if the child is not making expected progress; if the child is making more progress than expected; if the child is not accessing accommodations or services; if the child is absent a lot, or sick, or there is any meaningful change.
- Take a deep breath and smile. You've done your best. You have an amazing opportunity to serve students and provide excellent education for all—and you are doing exactly that!

96

Acronyms and other useful terms

ADD/ADHD	Attention deficit disorder; attention deficit hyperactivity disorder
e.g.	for example
FCR	Federal Code of Regulations (the regulations)
504	Section 504 of the Rehabilitation Act of 1973
IDEA	Individuals with Disabilities Education Improvement Act
i.e.	that is
IEE	Independent Education Evaluation
IEP	Individualized Education Program
LEA	local educational agency; generally, the school district
OCR	Office for Civil Rights of the US Department of Education
OSEP	Office for Special Education Programs
OSERS	Office for Special Education Rehabilitative Services
SLD	Specific learning disability
SWD	students with disabilities
USC	United States Code (the law)

97

Bibliography/Cases

Alvin Independent School District v. A.D., 48 IDELR 240 (5ᵗʰ Cir. 2007).

Ashli and Gordon C. v. State of Hawaii, 47 IDELR 65 (D. HI. 2007).

Axelrod v. Phillips Academy, 30 IDELR 516 (D. MA 1999).

Board of Education of Hendrick Hudson Central School District v. Rowley, 458 U.S. 176 (1982).

Board of Education of Montgomery County v. S.G., 47 IDELR 285 (4ᵗʰ Cir. 2007).

Board of Education of Township High School District No. 211 v. Ross, 47 IDELR 241, 486 F.3d 267 (7ᵗʰ Cir. 2007).

Brillon v. Klein Independent School District, 41 IDELR 121 (5ᵗʰ Cir. 2004).

C.G. and B.S. v. Five Town Community School District, 49 IDELR 93 (1ˢᵗ Cir. 2008).

Clovis (CA) Unified School District, 47 IDELR 58 (SEA CA 2006).

Community Independent School District, 42 IDELR 244 (SEA TX 2004).

Cordiero v. Driscoll, 47 IDELR 189 (D. MA 2007).

Deal v. Hamilton County Board of Education, 42 IDELR 109 (6ᵗʰ Cir. 2004); 49 IDELR 123 (6ᵗʰ Cir. 2008).

Derek B. v. Donegal School District, 47 IDELR 34 (E. D. PA 2007).

Doe v. Board of Education of the Tullahoma City Schools, 20 IDELR 617 (6ᵗʰ Cir. 1993).

E. M. v. Pajaro Valley Unified School District, 48 IDELR 39 (N. D. CA 2007).

98

E.P. v. San Ramon Valley Unified School District, 48 IDELR 66, 2007 WL 1795747 (N.D. Cal. 2007).

Edinburg (TX) Consolidated Independent School District, 49 IDELR 170 (OCR 2007).

Ellenberg v. New Mexico Military Institute, 47 IDELR 153, 478 F.3d 1262 (10th Cir. 2007).

Elmhurst School District 205, 46 IDELR 25 (SEA IL 2006).

Fisher v. Board of Education of the Christina School District , 41 IDELR 238 (DEL 2004).

Fuhrmann v. East Hanover Boad of Education, 993 F. 2d 1031; 19 IDELR 1065 (3rd Cir. 1993).

G.D. v. Westmoreland School District, 930 F.2d 942 (1st Cir. 1991).

Goleta Union Elementary School District v. Ordway, 38 IDELR 64 (D. CA 2002).

Grim v. Rhinebeck Central School District, 346 F. 3d 377 (2nd. Cir. 2003).

Heather S. v. Wisconsin, 125 F. 3D 1045, 26 IDELR 870 (7th Cir. 1997).

Hjortness v. Neenah Joint School District, 48 IDELR 119 (7th Cir. 2007).

Hood v. Encinitas Union School District, 47 IDELR 213, 486 F.3d 1099 (9th Cir. 2007).

Houston Independent School District v. Bobby R., 31 IDELR 185, 200 F. 3d 341 (5th Cir. 2000).

Independent School District No. 281 v. Minnesota Department of Education, 48 IDELR 222 (MN App. Ct. 2007).

J.L. v. Mercer Island School District, 46 IDELR 273 (W. D. WA 2006).

Jaffess v. Council Rock School District, 46 IDELR 246 (D. E. PA 2006).

99

Jefferson County School District R-1, (SEA CO 2003).

L. M. v. Department of Education, State of Hawaii, 46 IDELR 100 (D. HI 2006).

Lachman v. Illinois Board of Education, 441 IDELR 156, 852 F. 2d 290 (7th Cir. 1988).

Leighty by Leighty v. Laurel School District, 48 IDELR 214 (D. W. PA 2006).

Letter to Clarke, 48 IDELR 77 (OSEP 2007).

Letter to McKethan, 25 IDELR 295 (OCR 1995).

M.S. v. Mullica Township Board of Education, 49 IDELR 154 (3rd Cir. 2008).

Mr. and Mrs. M. v. Ridgefield Board of Education, 47 IDELR 258 (D. CT 2007).

Mr. G. v. Timberlane Regional School District, 47 IDELR 5 (D. NH 2007).

Mr. I v. Maine School Administrative District No. 55, 47 IDELR 121, 480 F.3d 1 (1st Cir. 2007)

Middlesex Borough Board of Education, 38 IDELR 232 (SEA NJ 2003).

Montgomery Township Board of Education , 43 IDELR 186 (3rd Cir. 2005).

Murray v. Montrose County School District, 51 F. 3d 921 (10th Cir. 1995).

OCR Senior Staff Memorandum, 19 IDELR 894 (OCR 1992).

PGA Tour Inc. v. Casey Martin, 121 S. Ct. 1879 (2001).

Pachl v. Seagren, 46 IDELR 1 (8th Cir. 2006).

100

Park v. Anaheim Union High School District, 444 F. 3d 1149; 45 IDELR 178 (9th Cir. 2006) (reversed; remanded on other issues, 464 F. 3d 1025; 46 IDELR 151 (9th Cir. 2006).

Pierce v. Mason City School District, 48 IDELR 7 (S.D. OH 2007).

Roland M.v. Concord School Committee, 16 IDELR 1129 (1st Cir. 1990).

Shelby County (TN) School District, 45 IDELR 259 (OCR 2005).

Sherman and Nishanian v. Mamaroneck Union Free School District, 39 IDELR 181 (2nd Cir. 2003).

Somoza v. New York City Department of Education, 47 IDELR 127 (D. S. NY 2007).

Strock v. Independent School District No. 281, 49 IDELR 273 (D. MN 2008).

T. B. and E.B. v. Warwick School Committee, et al., 361 F. 3rd 80; 40 IDELR 253 (1st Cir. 2004).

T. S. v. Board of Education of the Town of Ridgefield, 10 F. 3d 87, 20 IDELR 889 (2nd. Cir. 1993).

T. W. v. Unified School District # 259, 43 IDELR 187 (10th Cir. 2005).

Timberlane Regional School District, 45 IDELR 139 (SEA NH 2006).

Watson v.Kingston City School District, 43 IDELR 244 (2nd Cir. 2005).

West Windsor-Plainsboro Regional School District Board of Education, 44 IDELR 159 (D.C. N. J. 2005).

Winston-Salem/Forsyth County Board of Education, 43 IDELR 267 (SEA NC 2005).

101

BOOKS/PAPERS/WEBSITES/OTHER SOURCES

Dealing with Difficult People, Christina Osborne, DK Publishing, Inc. (New York, New York, 2002).

Essential Facilitation for Individualized Education Program Meetings, Interaction Institute for Social Change, JDL and Associates, LLC.

Getting to YES, Roger Fisher, William Ury, and Bruce Patton; The Program on Negotiation at Harvard Law School, http://www.pon.harvard.edu

Grades, Report Cards, Etc….and the Law, Miriam Kurtzig Freedman, www.SchoolLawPro.com; Miriam@schoollawpro.com (2008).

IEP and Inclusion Tips for Parents and Teachers, Ann Eason and Kathy Whitbread. Available at www.wrightslaw.com/store and www.amazon.com.

Leading Successful IEP Teams: A Guide to Managing the People and the Process, Gerry Klor (LRP Publications, www.lrp.com).

Managing Meetings, Tim Hindle, Essential Managers, DK Publishing, Inc. (New York, New York, 1998).

Meeting NCLB's Mandates: Your Quick-Reference Guide to Assessments and Accountability, Miriam Kurtzig Freedman, M.A., J.D., LRP Publications (2008). www.lrp.com.

Say the Right Thing: A Guide for Responding to Parents' IEP Requests, Gerry Klor, LRP Publications (2007).

Student Testing and the Law, Miriam Kurtzig Freedman, LRP Publications. www.lrp.com.

"Things that "Go Bump" in the Meeting, Nancy Kolb, Professional Development, CASE/EDCO/LABBB, Waltham, MA.

Some good websites: www.ed.gov; www.lrp.com; www.schoollawpro.com; www.wrightslaw.com.

And others? Your favorites? Let us know! Email Miriam at Miriam@schoollawpro.com.

102

About the author, MIRIAM KURTZIG FREEDMAN, M.A., J.D.

Attorney Miriam Kurtzig Freedman works with people who want better schools and helps practitioners move from confusion to **confidence** when dealing with legal requirements. Why? So they can get back to the mission of educating ALL children.

Miriam, a school attorney, is of counsel to the Boston law firm of Stoneman, Chandler & Miller LLP. She provides clients and national audiences with lively and practical keynotes, training, and consultation. Her entertaining presentations are in "plain English" and promote best practices among her audiences. A former teacher, Miriam "gets" it--what school folks need to know and do.

Miriam co-founded Special Education Day (celebrated annually on December 2) and the Special Education Day Committee (SPEDCO) to spur special education reform. info@specialeducationday.com. She is a member of the National Speakers Association, the Education Consumer Consultants Network, and the Massachusetts Bar Association. A summary of her writing, speaking, and consulting experience is available at: www.schoollawpro.com.

She received her law degree from New York University, masters from the State University of New York, Stony Brook, and bachelor of arts from Barnard College (Columbia University). During the winter term, Miriam is a visiting fellow at Stanford University.

103

For Further Information

.....please contact Miriam
at Stoneman, Chandler & Miller LLP

617 542-6789
Miriam@SchoolLawPro.com
www.schoollawpro.com

Thank you for the important work you do!

*Together—moving from confusion to confidence
to get back to the mission of educating ALL children*